Play Ball!

by Joseph Benjamin

Here is a big ball.
The ball is round.

You can kick this ball.
You can play with it.

Here is a big ball.
This ball is round, too.

You can bounce
this ball.
You can play with it.

Here is a big ball.
The ball is **not** round.

You can play
with this ball.
You can run
with it, too.

You can play
a game
with a ball
at school.

You can play
with a ball
at home, too.